CODE READER™

Making Difficult Words Easy

Code Reader Books provide codes with "sound keys" to help read difficult words. For example, a word that may be difficult to read is "unicorn," so it might be followed by a code like this: unicorn *(YOO-nih-korn)*. By providing codes with phonetic sound keys, Code Reader Books make reading easier and more enjoyable.

Examples of Code Reader™ Keys

Long a sound (as in make):
a *(with a silent e)* or **ay**
Examples: able *(AY-bul)*; break *(brake)*

Short i sound (as in sit): **i** or **ih**
Examples: myth *(mith)*; mission *(MIH-shun)*

Long i sound (as in by):
i *(with a silent e)* or **y**
Examples: might *(mite)*; bicycle *(BY-sih-kul)*

Keys for the long o sound (as in hope):
o *(with a silent e)* or **oh**
Examples: molten *(MOLE-ten)*; ocean *(OH-shen)*

Codes use dashes between syllables *(SIH-luh-buls)*, and stressed syllables have capital letters.

To see more Code Reader sound keys, see page 44.

SINKING OF THE TITANIC

TREASURE BAY

Sinking of the Titanic
A Code Reader™ Book
Blue Series

Reading Consultant: Jennifer L. VanSlander, Ph.D., Asst. Professor of Educational Leadership, Columbus State University

Code Reader™ is a trademark of Treasure Bay, Inc.

Patent Pending.
Code Reader books are designed using an innovative system of methods to create and include phonetic codes to enhance the readability of text. Reserved rights include any patent rights.

Published by
Treasure Bay, Inc.
PO Box 519
Roseville, CA 95661 USA

Printed in China

Library of Congress Control Number: 2024944970

ISBN: 978-1-60115-729-4

Visit us online at:
CodeReader.org

PR-1-25

CONTENTS

4.14.

The night of April 14, 1912, was clear and cold. Stars reflected off the waters of the North Atlantic. But the moon was not visible. The *RMS Titanic (ty-TAN-ik)* steamed through the ocean *(OH-shun)* on day five of her first, or maiden, voyage *(VOY-ej)*. The new ship was the largest in the world. By 11:40 p.m., some passengers *(PAS-en-jurs)* slept in their cabins. Others played cards or visited in the ship's lounges *(LOWN-jez)*. Some listened to the orchestra *(OR-kes-trah)*. Few ventured *(VEN-churd)* on deck. The temperature had dropped to 32 degrees.

1912

High up the mast, a lookout sat in the **crow's nest**. He kept careful watch for icebergs *(ISE-burgz)*. But it was hard to see in the dark. Suddenly, something loomed in front of *Titanic*. The lookout called down to the bridge, "Iceberg, right ahead!" First Officer William Murdoch *(MUR-dok)* tried to turn the ship. But it was too late. The iceberg scraped along the ship's hull. Within three hours, the ship would sink to the bottom of the ocean.

ACROSS THE SEA

Only 100 years before *Titanic*, the trip from Europe *(YUR-up)* to North America had been difficult and dangerous *(DANE-jur-us)*. It required *(ree-KWY-urd)* sailing the storm-tossed North Atlantic. The sea often rose into huge swells. Harsh winds threatened to push ships off course. Thick fog made navigation *(nav-ih-GAY-shun)* almost impossible at times. Icebergs floated into shipping lanes. These dangers led to many shipwrecks *(SHIP-reks)*. In the early 1800s, as many as 4 out of every 25 ships never made it to their destinations *(des-tih-NAY-shunz)*. Those that did often took a month or more to make the crossing.

Life on a ship was often uncomfortable *(un-KUM-fur-tuh-bul)*. Passengers faced crowded and stuffy conditions *(kun-DIH-shunz)*. Third-class passengers were crammed into the lowest levels of ships. Many of these people were emigrants *(EM-ih-grents)*—people leaving their homeland to make a new life in America.

Crossing the Atlantic during the 1800s took between 6 and 14 weeks, depending on wind and weather conditions.

Firemen, or stokers, shoveled 825 tons of coal into Titanic's boilers daily, dumping 100 tons of ash into the ocean. The coal burned in hot furnaces that boiled water into steam and powered the ship's propellers.

MAURETANIA
(maw-ruh-TAY-nee-uh)

However, many emigrants died of disease *(dih-ZEEZ)* or starvation *(star-VAY-shun)* before the sailing ship made it to America.

In the mid-1800s, steamships began crossing the Atlantic. Instead of sails, these ships were powered by steam engines *(EN-jinz)*. Coal was burned in boilers to generate *(JEN-uh-rate)* steam. The steam powered an engine that turned a propeller in the water.

By the late 1800s, more people were crossing the Atlantic than ever before. Shipping companies began to compete for their business *(BIZ-ness)*. Among the biggest shipping lines were White Star, Cunard *(KYOO-nard)*, and Hamburg-Amerika. These companies raced to build *(bild)* bigger, faster, more luxurious *(lux-ZHUR-ee-us)* ships. Their ships became known for their impressive safety records. In 1911, the *New York Times* stated that modern ships would stay afloat after the "most violent *(VY-oh-lent)* shock."

In 1907, Cunard *(KYOO-nard)* introduced the *Lusitania (loo-suh-TAY-nee-uh)* and *Mauretania (maw-ruh-TAY-nee-uh)*. These ships were the biggest and fastest ever built *(bilt)*.

3.31.1909

Keel laid for *Titanic*

Each stretched 790 feet. They could travel at 26 to 28 knots. That is about 30 to 32 miles per hour. At this speed, the ships could cross the Atlantic in less than five days.

White Star chairman, J. Bruce Ismay *(IZ-mee)*, wanted to keep up with his competitors *(kum-PEH-tih-turz)*. He decided not to try to set a speed record. Instead, White Star would build the largest, most luxurious *(lux-ZHUR-ee-us)* ships on the ocean. The ships would be the *Olympic (oh-LIM-pik)*, *Titanic (ty-TAN-ik)*, and *Gigantic (jy-GAN-tik)*.

White Star's ships were built by the shipbuilder with the largest operation *(op-er-AY-shun)* in the world. It was located in Belfast, Northern Ireland.

The keel for *Titanic* was laid on March 31, 1909. This formed the ship's spine. Next, the ship's bottom, or hull, was built. Steel beams attached to the keel formed a frame for the ship. The frame was covered with more than 2,000 steel plates. The plates were held together by heated steel pins called rivets. Some of the rivets were pounded into place by hand. A giant hydraulic *(hy-DRAW-lik)*, or water-powered, riveter secured *(seh-KYURD)* others.

The ship builder altered its shipyards with larger piers (peerz) and other structures (STRUK-churz) to make room for Titanic and Olympic.

As roughly 3,000 men constructed Titanic over a period *(PEER-ree-ud)* of 26 months, 8 deaths and 246 injuries occurred *(uh-KURD)*.

By May 31, 1911, *Titanic's* frame was complete. Nearly 100,000 people watched as the ship was launched *(LAWN-cht)*. But the inside of the ship wasn't done yet. The *Titanic* was moved to a deep-water wharf *(worf)*. It spent the next 10 months there as builders completed it. Three engines were added. They would be powered by 29 boilers. Four funnels rose above the deck. Three served as smokestacks. The fourth was added to make the ship look balanced. It also provided ventilation *(vent-til-LAY-shun)*. Cabins, dining rooms, and decks were painted and furnished.

By the time it was completed, *Titanic* stretched 882.75 feet and was 92.5 feet wide. It was as long as three football fields! From the bottom of the keel to the top of the funnels, the ship towered 175 feet. It weighed *(wade)* 46,329 tons.

Titanic was ready to sail.

NOW THAT'S BIG

Everything about *Titanic* was huge *(hyooj)*. Its engines were the largest of their kind ever built. Each was nearly 40 feet tall, or about as high as a four-story building. The two outer propellers were each more than 23 feet in diameter *(dy-AM-uh-tur)*. The center propeller measured 16 feet across. Each of *Titanic's* 29 boilers could fit a double-decker bus inside. The ship's 3 anchors *(ANG-kurz)* weighed more than 15 tons apiece

MAIDEN VOYAGE

Titanic left Belfast on April 2, 1912. She sailed to Southampton *(sowth-HAMP-tun)*, England. There she would take on passengers for her maiden voyage. On the way to Southampton, the crew inspected *Titanic's* lifeboats. The ship carried 16 wooden lifeboats. It also had four collapsible *(kuh-LAP-sih-bul)* boats. These had canvas sides. The 20 boats could hold a total of 1,178 people. That was only half the number of people who would sail on *Titanic's* maiden voyage. But regulations *(reg-yoo-LAY-shunz)* did not require the vessel to provide emergency *(ee-MUR-jen-see)* lifeboats for even that many.

No one thought the lifeboats would be needed. In its advertising *(AD-ver-tize-ing)*, White Star wrote about the ship's 16 watertight areas *(AIR-ee-uz)* or compartments. In an accident *(AK-sih-dent)*, the compartments could be sealed off. This would prevent other areas of the ship from flooding *(FLUH-ding)*. Even with two compartments flooded *(FLUD-ed)*, *Titanic* would remain afloat.

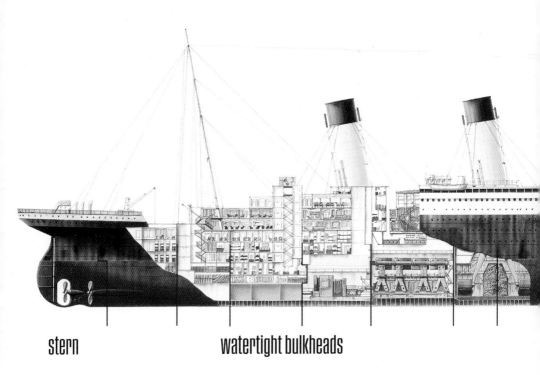

stern   watertight bulkheads

The watertight doors could be closed from the bridge *(bridzh)*. All it took was the flip of a switch. The watertight doors were supposed to make the vessel "practically unsinkable."

Passengers began to board *Titanic* on April 10. Many wealthy *(WEL-thee)* people traveled in first class. Among them were American businessmen John Jacob Astor and Isidor Straus *(IZ-uh-dohr STROWS)*. Second class was filled with less wealthy families. Third class held the cheapest-ticket holders and included hundreds of emigrants. These emigrants spoke many languages *(LANG-wuh-juz)*, including French, Polish *(POH-lish)*, and Chinese *(CHY-neez)*.

Titanic *was equipped with many spaces to relax, including a swimming pool, a gymnasium (jim-NAY-zee-um), and a Parisian (par-EE-zhen) café (caf-AY).*

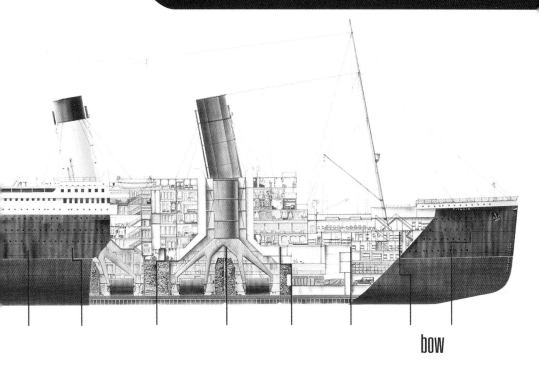

bow

The captain for *Titanic's* first voyage was Edward J. Smith. About 900 crew members kept the ship running. Some served as waiters or stewards. Others worked as firemen. They kept the boilers burning to provide steam for the engines. There were also cooks, bellboys, engineers *(en-jen-EERZ)*, and musicians *(myoo-ZISH-unz)*.

The ship's designer *(dee-ZINE-er)*, Thomas Andrews, also boarded. So did White Star chairman J. Bruce *(broos)* Ismay *(IZ-mee)*.

NARROW MISS

As *Titanic* steamed out of Southampton's port, her propellers churned up the water. The waves rocked the *SS New York*, a smaller ship tied up nearby. The lines tying the *SS New York* to the dock snapped. The smaller ship began drifting toward *Titanic*. Tugboats managed to grab the *New York's* lines. Captain Smith increased *Titanic's* speed. The two ships narrowly *(NARE-oh-lee)* avoided *(uh-VOYD-ud)* a collision. If they had crashed, *Titanic* wouldn't have sailed on April 10.

On April 5, 1912, *Titanic was open to the paying public for tours while docked at Southampton.*

Titanic sailed from Southampton at noon on April 10. From there, the ship made stops in France *(frans)* and Ireland. More passengers boarded at each stop. Nearly 1,325 passengers would take part in the maiden voyage. Counting the crew, the ship carried about 2,220 people.

On Friday, April 12, *Titanic* steamed into the open ocean. Smith set the ship's course *(kors)* for New York. The sea was smooth.

Titanic quickly picked up speed. Soon she was making 22 knots (25.3 miles per hour). Ismay *(IZ-mee)* began to talk of reaching New York earlier *(UR-lee-ur)* than planned.

As the ship sped along, passengers explored her many decks. First-class passengers enjoyed fine restaurants *(REST-uh-RAWNTZ)*. They swam in the indoor pool. Some exercised *(EK-sur-SIZED)* in the gym *(jim)*.

First-class passengers paid as much as $4,350 (which would be like paying more than $100,000 today) for a two-bedroom parlor suite (sweet).

The design *(dee-ZINE)* style of *Titanic* was meant to give the impression *(im-PRESH-un)* of a modern, high-class hotel instead of a ship.

First-class passengers slept in large cabins with private *(PRY-vet)* bathrooms. Second and third-class passengers were not allowed *(uh-LOWD)* in first-class areas. But they enjoyed nice spaces in their parts of the ship. Their cabins were roomier than on most vessels. The public areas were large and comfortable. The food was tasty *(TAYS-tee)*.

By Sunday evening, *Titanic* had reached the cold waters south of Newfoundland *(NOO-fund-lund)*, Canada *(KAN-uh-duh)*. Throughout *(throo-OWT)* the day, other ships in the area had sent *Titanic* six ice warnings. The radio *(RAY-dee-oh)* operators *(OP-er-ay-terz)* wrote down the warnings. But they set some of them aside. They were busy sending passengers' messages. They passed other reports on to the captain and crew. No one seemed worried. Captain Smith posted extra lookouts that night. But he kept the ship moving at full speed.

After the collision (kuh-LIH-zhun), water began filling six of the ship's 16 watertight compartments, and the vessel sank in less than three hours.

"Those of the crew who were asleep in their bunks turned out, and we all rushed on deck to see what was the matter. We found the ship had struck an iceberg, as there was a large quantity (KWAN-tih-tee) of ice . . . on the starboard (STAR-burd) side of the foredeck. We did not think it very serious (SEER-ee-us) so went below again, cursing the iceberg for disturbing us."

Joseph Scarrott *(SCARE-rut),* Titanic *crew member*

At 11:40 p.m., a lookout in the crow's nest spotted an iceberg. It was less than a half a mile away. It towered directly in front of the ship. At *Titanic's* speed, it would take a mile to turn. But First Officer Murdoch *(MUR-dok)* tried anyway. At the same time, he flipped the switch that closed the water-tight doors. A little more than 30 seconds later, the iceberg scraped *Titanic's* hull. It tore into at least 5 of *Titanic's* watertight compartments in only 10 seconds.

THE UNSINKABLE SINKS

Most passengers barely even noticed *(NOH-tist)* the impact. Some said it seemed as if the boat had struck a log. Others said it felt like "rolling over a thousand *(THOW-zand)* marbles." Those closer to the impact experienced *(ex-PEER-ree-enst)* a violent jolt. One steward recalled hearing "a rending, crunching, ripping sound."

Some passengers ignored the bump. Those more curious *(KYUR-ee-us)* went up to the deck to explore. Some found pieces *(PEE-sez)* of ice there. But even then, they did not worry. They believed the ship was unsinkable. As one said, the "ship could smash a hundred icebergs and not feel it." Crew members reassured *(ree-uh-SHURD)* passengers everything was fine. They continued *(kun-TIN-yood)* their work polishing brass or setting tables. They told people to go back to bed.

The first touch (tuch) of our lifeboat on that black sea came to me as a last goodbye to life, and so we put off—a tiny boat on a great sea—rowed away from what had been a safe home for five days. . . . I thought the danger (DANE-jur) must be exaggerated (ex-ZA-juh-ray-tid), and we could all be taken aboard again. But surely the outline of that great, good ship was growing less."

Elizabeth Shutes, first-class passenger as governess to Miss Edith Graham *(gram)*

Captain Smith and ship designer *(dee-ZINE-er)* Thomas Andrews inspected the damage. They found water pouring into five (and then a sixth) of the ship's watertight compartments. Andrews realized the ship couldn't stay afloat. The weight of the water in the compartments would pull the bow, or front, of the ship down. As the bow sank, water would reach the top of the watertight compartments. The compartments did not extend to the upper levels of the ship. Water would flow over the top of one compartment and into the next.

At 12:05 a.m., Smith told the crew to order passengers into lifeboats. At first, many refused *(ree-FYOOZD)*. Most believed the boats were being loaded only as a precaution *(pree-KOSH-un)*. They felt safer aboard *Titanic* than in a tiny lifeboat.

Some passengers thought the evacuation (ee-VAK-yoo-AY-shun) was just a drill; in the confusion (kun-FYOO-zhun), it took more than an hour to launch (lawnch) the first boat.

Titanic lifeboat occupancy

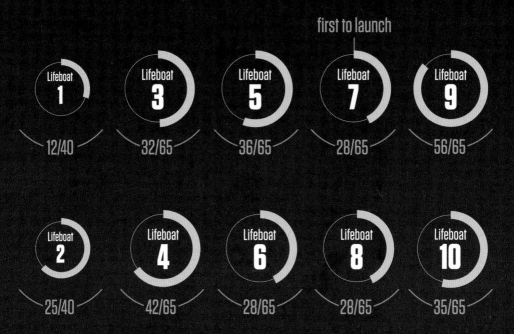

first to launch

| Lifeboat 1 | Lifeboat 3 | Lifeboat 5 | Lifeboat 7 | Lifeboat 9 |
| 12/40 | 32/65 | 36/65 | 28/65 | 56/65 |

| Lifeboat 2 | Lifeboat 4 | Lifeboat 6 | Lifeboat 8 | Lifeboat 10 |
| 25/40 | 42/65 | 28/65 | 28/65 | 35/65 |

Others made their way to the boat deck. There, lifeboats hung 70 feet above the icy *(I-see)* Atlantic. Officers loaded women and children onto the lifeboats. Some officers allowed men to enter the boats if there were not enough women and children to fill them. Others refused to allow men into the boats. The first lifeboat was lowered at 12:45 a.m. It carried only 28 people. It could have held 65. Many other lifeboats were also lowered *(LOH-wurd)* when only halfway full. Some crew members feared the boats would break if they were too full. Most of the people loaded into the lifeboats early on were first-class passengers. Third-class passengers were told to wait at the foot of a staircase. Crew members said they would get further instructions *(in-STRUK-shunz)* soon.

In the radio room, *Titanic's* two radio operators sent out distress

Gray numbers show the number of passengers on each lifeboat compared to how many people each lifeboat was designed to carry.

Lifeboat 11 — 70/65
Lifeboat 13 — 65/65
Lifeboat 15 — 65/65
Lifeboat A — 12/47
Lifeboat C — 43/47
Lifeboat 12 — 30/65
Lifeboat 14 — 58/65
Lifeboat 16 — 40/65
Lifeboat B — 21/47
Lifeboat D — 25/47

calls. A total of 23 ships were crossing the Atlantic that night. Most were too far away to help. The closest ship to respond was Carpathia *(kar-PAY-thee-uh)*. It was 67 miles away. The ship immediately *(im-MEE-dee-ut-lee)* changed course to steam toward the sinking *Titanic*.

The last wooden lifeboats were lowered *(LOH-erd)* shortly before 2 a.m. The bow was now almost completely underwater.

The final lifeboats had to be lowered only 15 feet to reach the water's surface *(SUR-fus)*. The crew tried to set up the collapsible *(cuh-LAP-suh-bul)* lifeboats. Third-class passengers were finally *(FINE-uh-lee)* allowed onto the deck. Many of them tried to climb into the collapsible boats. Two of the boats made it into the water.

THE UNSINKABLE SINKS

Only about 40 of the people who jumped or found an overturned lifeboat survived in the freezing water.

Before the final two collapsible boats could be filled, *Titanic's* bow lurched forward *(FOR-wurd)* and down. From inside came crashing noises. Those were the sounds of refrigerators *(ree-FRIJ-er-ay-terz)*, boilers, and other heavy items smashing through the ship. The stern, or back, of the ship rose nearly straight out of the water. The back railing towered 250 feet above the ocean. Some passengers fell or jumped into the frigid water below. The weight *(wate)* of

"We could see groups of the almost 1,500 people still aboard, clinging in clusters or bunches, like swarming bees; only to fall in masses, pairs, or alone, as the great after-part of the ship, 250 feet of it, rose into the sky. . . . Here it seemed to pause (pawz), and just hung, for what felt like minutes."

Jack B. Thayer, first-class passenger on overturned lifeboat.

the stern was too much. The ship split in two. The bow slowly sank out of sight (site). The stern settled back into a level position (puh-ZISH-un). Water rushed into its torn-off front. Within minutes, the stern tilted forward. Then it slowly sank.

By 2:20 a.m., the unsinkable ship was gone.

After the ship slipped beneath the waves, Titanic's *resting place remained a mystery (MIS-ter-ee) until 1985.*

SINKING OF TITANIC
Timeline

11:39 P.M. Lookout reports an iceberg in *Titanic's* path.

11:40 P.M. *Titanic* strikes the iceberg, which tears *(tairz)* through the ship's watertight compartments.

12:05 A.M. Captain Smith gives the order to ready the lifeboats and start loading.

12:25 A.M. *Carpathia (kar-PAY-thee-uh)* responds to emergency broadcast *(BRAWD-cast)* and changes course.

12:45 A.M. The first lifeboat (containing only 28 people) is lowered.

2:00 A.M. Collapsible lifeboats are set up for third-class passengers.

2:20 A.M. After splitting in two, *Titanic* sinks below the waves.

4:10 A.M. *Carpathia* arrives and begins evacuating *(ee-VAK-yoo-AYT-ing)* survivors *(sur-VY-verz)* from the lifeboats.

8:50 A.M. With more than 700 survivors aboard, *Carpathia* heads for New York.

REMEMBERING TITANIC

As *Titanic* sank, roughly 700 people watched from lifeboats. More than 1,500 others went down with the ship. Some drowned. But some now floated in their life jackets in the 28-degree seawater. They cried out for help. Two or three lifeboats returned to pull people out of the water. But the other usable *(YOOZ-uh-bul)* lifeboats stayed away. Those aboard feared they would be swamped if they tried to pick up survivors.

Around dawn, *Carpathia* arrived. The ship had steamed at top speed through the dark to reach *Titanic*. *Carpathia's* crew helped just over 700 survivors from the lifeboats aboard. Everyone still in the water was dead.

With *Titanic's* survivors onboard, *Carpathia* headed back to New York. It arrived on April 18. People around the world were stunned at news of the disaster *(dih-ZAS-ter)*.

Lifeboat 2, which was about half full, was the first boat to reach Carpathia in the morning of April 15.

SURVIVAL BY THE NUMBERS

Survival *(sur-VY-vul)* aboard *Titanic* depended largely *(LARJ-lee)* on class. More first-class passengers survived than died. In contrast, 75 percent of all third-class passengers died. About 75 percent of the crew went down with the ship as well. All eight band members aboard *Titanic* died after playing as the ship sank. Captain Smith, First Officer Murdoch, and ship designer Thomas Andrews also went down with *Titanic*.

Survival Ratio by Class

1ST

57 / 175 Men
140 / 144 Women
5 / 6 Children

2ND

14 / 168 Men
80 / 93 Women
24 / 24 Children

3RD

75 / 462 Men
76 / 165 Women
27 / 79 Children

CREW

192 / 885 Men
20 / 23 Women

Many had seen the ship as a symbol *(SIM-bul)* of progress *(PRAH-gres)* and technology *(tek-NOL-uh-jee)*. They wondered how it could have sunk. A British inquiry *(IN-kwer-ee)* concluded that *Titanic* had been traveling too fast through waters known to hold icebergs.

After *Titanic*, several regulations *(reg-yoo-LAY-shunz)* were changed to improve safety at sea. Wireless operators were required to be on duty *(DOO-tee)* aboard all ships at all times. Each hour, all operators had to observe two periods of radio silence *(SY-lens)*. During this time, they listened for distress signals. The International *(in-ter-NASH-uh-nul)* Ice Patrol was also established. The patrol charted all ice in the North Atlantic. Lifeboat regulations were updated as well. Ships were required to carry enough lifeboats to accommodate *(uh-KOM-uh-date)* every person aboard.

Hercules (HUR-kyoo-leez) R.O.V.

Almost from the time *Titanic* sank people talked about finding the wreck. But navigation *(nav-ih-GAY-shun)* equipment *(ee-KWIP-ment)* at the time was not precise *(pree-SISE)*. No one knew the exact spot the ship had gone down. In addition, technology to explore deep underwater did not yet exist. By the early 1980s, scientists *(SY-un-tists)* had made advances in unmanned submersibles *(sub-MUR-sih-bulz)*. This allowed for exploration in deep waters. Several expeditions *(ex-puh-DISH-uns)* tried to locate the *Titanic*. In 1985, American oceanographer *(oh-shun-OG-ruh-fur)* Robert Ballard led a team to the North Atlantic. They discovered the wreck in 13,000 feet of water. The bow was mostly intact. But mud rose 60 feet up its hull. The stern lay 2,000 feet away. The extreme water pressure had crushed much of its structure *(STRUK-chur)* as it sank. Rust hung in formations that looked like icicles *(I-sik-ulz)*. Ballard called the formations "rusticles *(RUST-ik-ulz)*."

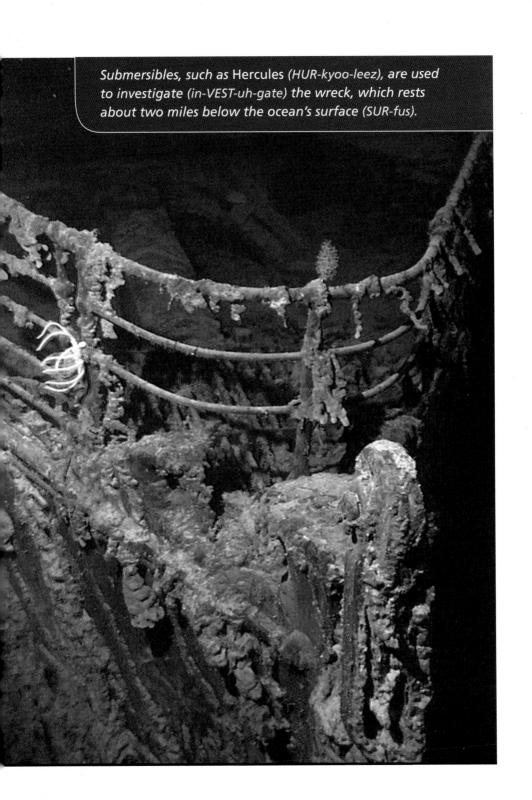

Submersibles, such as Hercules (HUR-kyoo-leez), are used to investigate (in-VEST-uh-gate) the wreck, which rests about two miles below the ocean's surface (SUR-fus).

Many items from Titanic, including menus (MEN-yooz), dishes, watches, and lighting fixtures, have been recovered for auction (AWK-shun) or display.

Over the years, additional *(ad-DISH-uh-nul)* expeditions *(ex-puh-DISH-uns)* have visited the wreck. Some have landed manned submersibles on *Titanic's* deck. Some have brought up metal from the hull. Tests on the metal have shown that the steel used to build *Titanic* contained high levels of sulfur. Builders at the time didn't know this could make steel brittle and apt to crack. The brittle steel may have shattered when the ship hit the iceberg.

Other explorers have searched the debris *(duh-BREE)* fields *(feeldz)* that surround the ship. Some have salvaged *(SAL-vejd)* materials from the seafloor. The company RMS Titanic, Inc., today has exclusive *(ex-KLOO-siv)* salvage rights to the ship. The organization has brought up more than 5,500 items. Among them are teacups, luggage, and statues *(STA-chooz)* that decorated the ship.

"The scientific (sy-en-TIF-ik) recovery and educational display of Titanic artifacts will broaden (BRAW-den) our knowledge (NAH-lej) of this magnificent ship, her passengers and crew, and the tragedy of her sinking. . . . The world wasn't black and white in 1912, and we shouldn't have to limit our understanding of the ship to historic photographs. Nothing is more compelling than seeing Titanic artifacts in three dimensions (dih-MEN-shunz)."

— Robert DiSogra, former president of Titanic International Society

Museums (myoo-ZEE-umz) in the United States, Canada, Ireland, and England have showcased artifacts and replicas from the ship.

Some people, including Ballard, do not think these items should be taken from the sea. They believe salvage operations dishonor (dis-ON-er) the Titanic and its victims. Others argue that salvaging preserves (pree-ZURVZ) the items. They say if the items are left on the seafloor, they will decay or be covered by sediment. They want to display the items as a way for the world to remember Titanic.

Such remembrance (ree-MEM-brans) also occurs through hundreds of books and films. Titanic memorials (meh-MOR-ee-ulz) in locations (loh-KAY-shunz) around the world draw visitors each year. More than 100 years have passed since the sinking of Titanic. But its story lives on.

GLOSSARY

crow's *(kroze)* **nest** a lookout platform located high on a ship's mast to allow for a good view of the surrounding sea

emigrants *(EM-ih-grents)* people moving from their homeland to a new country

exclusive *(ex-KLOO-siv)* belonging to only one person or group, not shared

hydraulic *(hy-DRAW-lik)* operated by the pressure created when water or another liquid is forced through a tube or other space

keel the main structure that supports a boat's frame and extends the full length of the boat's bottom

maiden involving the first attempt or act

pressure *(PREH-shur)* force exerted by pressing on an object or substance

salvaged *(SAL-vijd)* saved or recovered

sediment dirt or other materials that settle to the bottom of the ocean or another body of water

stewards people responsible for seeing to passengers' comfort aboard a ship, train, or airplane

submersibles *(sub-MUR-sih-bulz)* small vessels able to operate underwater, often to explore or carry out research

ventilation *(ven-tih-LAY-shun)* a system for providing a flow of fresh air